What is Bigger Than Anything?
(Infinity)

3rd Edition

by David E. McAdams

Copyright © 2025 Life is a Story Problem LLC. All rights reserved. No part of this work may be copied, stored or transmitted by any means without the express written consent of the copyright holder.

Other Books by David E. McAdams

Parrot Colors – A delightful introduction to colors featuring vibrant images of parrots. Perfect for ages 0-6.

Flower Colors – Explore the beauty of colors through captivating images of flowers. Ideal for ages 0-6.

Space Colors – Discover colors through stunning NASA space images. Suitable for ages 0-6.

People Colors – Introduces the concept of colors using diverse images of people from around the world. For ages 0-6.

If I Had a Monster – A charming story where monsters represent important people in a child's life. Fun for all ages.

Shapes – A playful introduction to geometric shapes, designed for children aged 3-6.

Numbers – A beginner-friendly book introducing the concept of numbers. Recommended for ages 5-7.

Redneck Number Book – A humorous and engaging way to learn numbers in a unique style. Great for ages 2-6.

What is Bigger Than Anything? (Infinity) – A fascinating look at the concept of infinity for curious minds aged 6-8.

Swing Sets (Set Theory) – A comprehensive introduction to set theory, tailored for students aged 7-10.

One Penny, Two – Join Jerry on his journey to buy a sports car as his penny doubles each day. A captivating read for ages 8-12.

Learning With Play Money Activity Kit – A fun hands-on kit to teach counting and large numbers with over $2,000,000 in play money. Best for ages 8-12.

My Favorite Fractals (Volumes 1 & 2) – A visual treat of high-resolution fractal images, appealing to all ages.

Even Generals Take Out the Garbage – A heartwarming story that teaches children the importance of doing chores. Suitable for young readers.

All Math Words Dictionary – A comprehensive math dictionary covering key concepts in pre-algebra, algebra, geometry, and pre-calculus.

The First Million Digits of Pi – A book containing the first million digits of pi, fascinating for math enthusiasts of all ages.

The First Million Digits of e – A collection of the first million digits of Euler's number (e). Engaging for all ages.

The Square Root of 2 to One Million Digits – Explore the first million digits of the square root of 2. For curious minds of all ages.

The First Hundred Thousand Prime Numbers – A handy reference featuring the first hundred thousand prime numbers, suitable for all ages.

Geometric Nets Project Book – Contains 80 geometric nets to copy, cut out, and assemble into 3D polyhedra. Ideal for ages 9 and up.

Geometric Nets Mega Project Book – Features 253 geometric nets to copy, cut out, and construct into 3D polyhedra. Suitable for ages 9 and up.

For an up-to-date list of books, visit https://www.DEMcAdams.com.

How big is big?

Are you big?

Are you big next to a rat?

Are you big next to an elephant?

Who is bigger, you or your daddy?

Which is bigger, your mommy or a house?

Which is bigger, a house or a city?

Which is bigger, a city or the world?

Which is bigger, the world or the solar system?

Which is bigger, a solar system or a galaxy?

What is bigger than anything?

Infinity means bigger than anything.

Can you count to 5?

Can you count one more than five? Six is one more than five.

Can you count one more than six? One more than six is seven.

You can always count 1 more than any number.

Archimedes said, "There is always one more number."

There is no last number, because there is always one more number.

Since there is no last number, numbers are infinite.

Infinity means more than any number you can imagine.

Can you imagine enough turtles to cover the whole world? Infinity is more than that.

Can you imagine how many stars are in a hundred billion galaxies? Infinity is more.

Infinity means more than any number.

Hands On Activity:

How big is infinity?

1. Take a piece of paper and a pencil. Start writing numeric digits on the paper.

2. How many numeric digits can you write on one piece of paper?

3. Each digit makes the number bigger. If you wrote numeric digits on paper for a whole day, would it be infinity?

4. No matter how many digits you write, it would not be infinity.

Words to know

Big   large compared to some standard

Bigger   larger than something

Infinite bigger or more than anything you might choose; not having an end.

Infinity the concept of not having an end

www.ingramcontent.com/pod-product-compliance
Lightning Source LLC
Chambersburg PA
CBHW050048080526
44586CB00014B/1515